DATE DUE

OCT 2 2 2007		

ALSO BY SARAH ARVIO

Visits from the Seventh

Sono

Sono

cantos

SARAH ARVIO

ALFRED A. KNOPF
NEW YORK   2006

THIS IS A BORZOI BOOK
PUBLISHED BY ALFRED A. KNOPF

www.aaknopf.com

Knopf, Borzoi Books, and the colophon are
registered trademarks of Random House, Inc.

Library of Congress Cataloging-in-Publication Data
Arvio, Sarah, [date].
Sono : cantos / Sarah Arvio.—1st ed.
p.   cm.
ISBN 0-307-26323-1
1. Rome (Italy)—Poetry.   I. Title.

PS3601.R78S66 2006
811'.6—dc22
2005044300

Printed in the United States of America
First Edition

Contents

Sono

Traveling

I'd been ostracized, so I hid my head.
And what was the view from under the sand;
it was a view of the Interior,

it was an Interior Ostracism.
It might have been a desert or a beach.
What if I said the world was my ostrich,

when I'd hoped to say it was my oyster;
what special muscle did I like to eat?
And what oyster was my sovereign world?

Spin the globe to Africa or Austin . . .
Was I a gawker, was I a creeper,
was I a stiltman, was I a sleeper?

Was this my world; it might be the oyster's.
Having it all in the palm of the hand
or in the palm at the end of the mind.

This was traveling and seeing the world;
there were verbs: to oyster and to ostrich.
Sand of the desert and sand of the sea,

each had its beauty, each had its place.
And yes, sand in the meat of the oyster,
and yes, sand in the meat of my own mind.

I gathered around it and made my pearl,
as pure as something made of grit can be.
This was Australia or Austerlitz;

here was an extravagant *ostrakon*
with the shell as the sky and the blue-and-
pink stain as sunset and the rim, what else,

as heaven. And this: lie in the desert
a little longer. Or sleep on the beach.
Then leave your shells behind you in the sand.

Matter

I was what mattered in the end. Or if
I didn't matter then nothing mattered,
and if I mattered, well then all things did.

O miracles and molecules, dust, rust.
It was always a matter of matter.
It might be meat or else it might be love

(if I was meat, if I was fit to eat).
What had never been matter would never
matter: you might say this was a moot point.

Clay and dust, ash and mud and mist and rust,
blood-orange sunsets and turning maples,
apples and cherries, sticks and trash and dust,

rumpled papers blowing across a street
(*dead letters sent to him that lives away*).
There was life, there was loss, there was no such

thing as loss—there was nothing that wasn't
both life and loss. No, it had to be said,
in questions of matter, nothing was lost.

It might be a matter of carnal love.
This was textual and material,
and for once the facts-of-the-matter were

both heartfelt and matter-of-fact. (Oh,
matter of course was always the mother.)
These were the facts of life, this was my life,

and there I was, right at the heart of it,
my own heart—at the heart-of-the-matter.
And did I matter now or in the end?

O mother, maintainer and measurer,
mud and fruit of the heart, meat of the heart,
the question might be asked, what was the end.

Fiesta

This much I found to say: I was afraid
facing the future to face the future.
What fool did I hope was my fortune, what

fortune or fact did I hope was my fool;
what fundament was wrong with my fortune.
Fashion me, I said, a fate I can fête,

fashion me a fate I don't have to hate,
diverting and no, never desperate,
and yes, find me a fund of fun, fun, fun

—a funicular not a funeral—
for going up, up, up and not down, down.
O phantom heart, phantasmagoria,

I had forgotten one word: forever.
A day, hello a flag, again a flag
wearing the colors of the inner heart.

Love, a forest of flags waving for me,
bending and blowing in the wind like flames,
a fiesta of flames burning for me,

turning and tossing in the wind like flags.
It was all such a factual feeling
and there was my fear in point of this fact.

It was a desire that had to be had,
actualized in a factual act.
The question arose, or the question fell:

was it no longer desire when it was had.
Oh fond, fond—fountain of my flames and flags,
a moment later it might have been had.

Green Market

The grocer was looking strangely at me.
Your aura, he said, pointing to my head:
you've got all the colors of the garden.

Radish and carrot, tulip and turnip,
some horticultural dynamism
in the arc of my ulterior glow.

A sovereign rarity, my soul rays,
spread out on my head like a color chart.
I matched the rainbow, the summer sunset,

the green flash, the lightning, the green-cheese moon.
—So was there a green market in heaven?
No, not at all, that was a blue market,

because blue was saved for the sea and sky,
blue was saved for the bottom of the soul:
in heaven they only ate blueberries.

What did I know, what could I ever know;
could I see the blue dark inside myself,
the dark occasion or my own third eye.

I could see the eye but never myself,
even with the help of a mirror or muse.
What use was vision if I couldn't see.

A celery stick might be nice with salt,
some celerity, some hilarity,
a sprig of parsley or a spinach leaf,

a green flag waving in the cosmic wind.
He'd learned to live, he said, without desire
(not an achievement for most of us). As

he gazed at my aura, I watched his eyes.
I saw desire; he was kidding himself
and maybe therefore he was kidding me.

Shadows

I saw some shadows moving on the wall
and heard a shuffle, as of wings or thoughts.
I rolled back the sheets and looked at the day,

a raw, blown day, white papers in the street.
Sheets were flapping in the sky of my mind,
I smelled the wet sheets, I tasted a day

in sheets hanging in the damp of a day.
White pages flapping: my life had been so new
when I didn't yet know how old it was.

I couldn't see the vistas on those sheets,
the dreamscapes sleeping deeply in those sheets;
I hadn't yet seen my shadow vita

or learned which host would trick me or treat me,
which of my hosts would give me something sweet,
some good counsel and a soft place to sleep,

or what was the name of my ghostwriter.
Who ghosted my life, whose dream would I ghost,
who wrote my name and date across these sheets,

and which sheets would be the wings of my thoughts,
and which would hold the words of my angels.
A host, and did I know I'd have a host;

no, a line of sheets is never a bed,
a gaggle of hosts is never a love,
a host is never as good as a home,

a ghost as good as a dog or a god.
But I had my heart, always had my heart
for god and a home as much as it hurt.

Roma

Though the home, we say, is where the heart is,
wonder if the heart is where the home is.
Had I found a heart for my home and did

I live there and love there: this was the point
that all roads should lead to if I traveled.
This was the question that was romanesque,

or else something random or romantic;
this was the ancient question of amor,
was it Rome and home and could I live there.

Here was a hurrah and a holiday,
all the domes planting a star in the sky,
all the domes pointing upward and somewhere,

all the crypts sinking downward and nowhere;
but did they point and did they also pierce,
did they crack the shadow or the sunshine.

Chiaroscuro of the coffered heart,
or the yes and no of the offered heart.
Did I fit with it, did it fit with me,

was I its shadow or its positive,
was I its pentacle or palindrome.
The point was to see there was no point

or was the arrow pointing to the heart,
a road sign, a feather or a weapon.
There was a dome and a home, there was Rome,

and for every recto there was verso.
We live to live and that's the most we know,
and then die to die and then it's over.

Thesaurus

Given a way would I be this; given
this thing would I be this. I never knew
how persons could be things, and yet we were

in the vast cosmic Thing; we were little
things. There were greater animations than
ourselves, and to them we were things. This was

a thought in the forest of—thesaurus
of—my nomenclature. How often had
I thought, am I alive or am I dead,

never knowing what either Thingness was.
These were the woods we were talking about,
these were the words we were talking about,

where the forest was always in the trees,
where what I saw was always what I was;
my words, some leaves, all bristling with my life,

animate and *aimée*, all that was all.
There was an aura, call it a halo,
call it the glow of the moment of grace;

there was something oracular and old,
there was the show and glow, there was hello,
there was yes, no, there was congenial

and genial and joy. There was genius,
a genie in the bottle, breath in the lungs,
there was more than just being as I was:

wind in the woods, a forest in my mind,
the mind of my life found in the forest,
the Thing being named my thing, as it was.

Grace

Somewhere over in the platonic place
where I was enshrined in my high ideal,
was there a pure depiction of myself

written in water or else on the wall,
a plural entity named for my grief
or named for my excursions into joy,

some Cerberus or trio of Graces
gracing my life with a howl or a dance,
some triangle of me, myself and I,

an altar to an alternating self
alone, alert beside the aqueduct—
an allusion to the trope of Sarah,

aleatory emblem of my all
as wind spit rain through the ancient arches
and cloud faces gleamed in the dark-lit sky.

There was now and then, there was yes and no,
there was gracious and there was also grave,
but was there a place for my gravity,

where the wall and the wind were in myself,
or a continuum of my own self,
graceful Cerberus, cerberean Grace

gravitating toward the heart of a want,
a place to create what I longed to be
—or the planet versus Platonism—

all the faces of my envisaged self,
engraved with weather, my wish and my will,
gravid with "luminous intensity."

Grief

So, was there something grand in all this grief,
some grand canyon or great cathedral vault,
some grand arcades and avenues and walls,

ringing with echoes, hello and goodbye,
the hoofs of centaurs and centurions.
The little griefs were the gauge of our lives,

the glass of water waiting to be drunk,
the stick of wood wanting to be knocked,
a sliver of glass, a splinter of wood.

Luck, luck, it was always the same lament,
what I never got and what I gave,
what I never gave and what I got.

I had always wanted to grace myself
with a garden growing before my eyes,
a riot of grandeur and abandon.

If you want a big thing, oh take a grave,
if you want a grand thing, oh take a life,
try out a garden, try out a grave.

Ha-ha ha-ha, there was the big guffaw,
a hundred halos and a hundred hells,
a great load of guff and a lot of gall;

there was Dada, there was Dionysus,
daimon, duende, a darling or a dog,
god and love, or a horse or a hope;

there we were, gaga at all forms of god,
there was godliness and there was a dog,
yipping at my heels, yippee oh yippee.

Scirocco

Was I allowed to be alive, was I
allocated to life, was I alive,
was I a specimen of the species:

these were the questions I asked myself
while the scirocco was thrashing the sky,
raining red leaves and raining orange sand.

Was I dust, dirt and sand, dare I be dust,
there in Africa where they swept me up
off the orange drifts of shoulders and hips,

off the drifting dunes where bodies were heaped,
lying in sleep, shifting in sleep and dream,
where I dreamed I was a specimen

born to be special and specialized,
as all specimens of the species were,
while dusk flames and dawn flames climbed on the dunes

in an ambience of rage artistry
or an arrangement of orange and red
artfully arising; was I dead or

alive; was this my allowance of life,
my own modicum of *become become*,
my scirocco my barocco of rage.

There were candle flames, there were cigarettes,
amber whiskeys, amphoras of *I am*,
there were amulets of *I am I am;*

there were orange flames, red leaves, orange sand,
moons, mornings; there were moments still to burn
back in Africa where they swept me up.

Flames

What might have ruined me, that I became,
rising, as they say, from ruins or flames
—gaudy flames of *I am I am I am*—

a fire of me refusing what I was
and watching that one self burn and become.
These were such flagrant and flamboyant words

—overblown, overburned words—but were true:
blue and green, flaring to yellow and red,
red flags, yellow rags, oh fluttering wings,

flaming some red-hot downright refusal.
With my hand reaching up against the sun
and taking the shape of a leaf or flame,

I blocked the light or I watched as it burned
around my splayed fingers or through the leaf.
All my words scorched in the heat of a fight,

leaf, leaf and flame, watching them rise and go,
goodbye, goodbye, preparing for hello;
all the hells lived, these could be my hellos,

all the hellions of the self I was.
Oh my dantesque demons, now say goodbye,
all the grandiose, grandiloquent griefs.

How sad to say goodbye to what I was,
also of course to what I might have been—
gorgeous glories going up and away.

Stage

Did I have a genie or a daimon
to usher me onstage or sweep me off,
my own dear harbinger or usherette?

Curtains! came a cry, and the curtains shook.
Here was a masquerade *en abîme*,
a hidden histrion hamming my lines

deep in the jewel box of my drama,
angeloform, deiform or magic.
O angels ruffling your wings in the wings,

which of you is my own special angel?
Why not have the courage of Coleridge
to say it was a dream or a vision;

it might be a wish or else an anguish,
it might be an image or a language.
Was it anecdotage or sabotage,

was it chanson or could it be chantage.
Historical or else hysterical
or else ancestral or angelical.

Was this the character I often shunned,
so sultry and desperate and ravaged;
was this the character I often wished,

oh my little magus oh my cabbage;
was this verbiage or genius or madness.
No rehearsals: you get only this chance,

one call for this life, one cue for this love
(know how to bow in and how to bow out),
you did it or you didn't, that's the play.

Grotesque

FOR SUSANNA MOORE

Freud had offered common unhappiness
but I know I wanted uncommon joy;
godly or ghostly, what help could be had,

was there a helping hand, was there a god.
There was grace, the only cure for grief,
the submission to the heart of your god,

to the heart or hand of a friend or god,
some giving in, the gift of giving in,
as common as the grackles and starlings.

As though hello could be a harbinger,
as though happiness could be happenstance,
saying holiday, saying holy day,

something lifting in the house of the heart.
And did I have a star, did I have a grail,
did I have the necessary grotto,

the grassy knoll, the grove, the granite bench,
for making my anguish into a wish,
for turning grief into grotesqueries—

meaning shape-shifters, meaning shadow art,
or hilarity in the house of god,
of god or the kings, that was my own house

if you believe the "thou" of the Quakers.
And all things that might shake or might quake,
as things did when they came into their own,

quiver and quake, and open in the air,
or burst a bud, or break an egg or seal,
or shake a frisky tail, or wave a crown.

Lessons

Hadn't I already learned my lessons,
by now didn't I know what I should know
for living a life? If only I had

learned what I should have or maybe unlearned
what I should never have known, if only
I had forgotten, lapsus, lull—limbo

between knowing and never having known,
though never knowing meant being new.
Laconic scholia of learned life,

undulating from newness to knownness.
There was no new lily, little person,
no new lily in the emperor's pond,

though the lilies kept budding and bursting.
There was no new life in the library,
except for my own, lurking there alone,

late or too late, as all the lessons were;
because the life-hour never came again,
"never to this life would it come again."

There was the island of the emperor
that lay inside the lily-padded pond,
there were the rest of us lilliputians

puttering near the limen of our god,
articulating and annotating.
Island, island, O pupil of the pond,

don't tell me the emperor wasn't god:
god might be a cloud or an emperor
and even god couldn't begin again.

Hope

I said this: would you give me back my hope
if I suffered hard enough, if I tried.
That hip-swinging hallelujah of hope,

that hip-hip-hooray we were talking about,
raying outward from the hip or the heart,
holistic, holy—those were all high things—

hyper-radical and hyper-real,
that gospel of helix and radiance.
Hail me, hail me, here I am alive,

falling from the lips of the lioness,
lambent and loved, gamboling like a lamb,
having gambled all my griefs and lost them.

Game of the gods, gamine of the cards,
inhaler of hashish and helium.
Here was the hub of the halo again,

the hub or nub of the halo or heart,
and the trope of turning to say hello;
we always said it "helio-hello."

Hello to the little girl and lambkin,
garrulous, hilarious, all grown up,
nibbling on nothing and feeling okay,

and sweetly holding hands with the harpist,
turning toward the sun, turning toward the sound
—my warp of the world, my harp of the heart—

sounding like myself, as I always sound,
snappy and stylish and too sonorous,
a little savage and a little sweet.

Cross

I was saying I never had a care,
meaning maybe that I was free of care,
or else meaning that no one cared for me,

but I loved all of you the same as me.
As the Christians said, love unto others,
love others if they believe as you do—

love them, my love, if they'll carry your cross,
crisscrossing the field of your destiny.
Neither Giambologna nor Morandi

is still making art in Bologna, though
they worshipped there at the altar of art
and then died in the service of their lord,

god of stillness and volatility.
By that was meant the art of moving air,
of sitting or lying down or flying,

a set of bottles or a pair of legs
standing or else hanging or lifting off,
or a field full of grasses and crosses.

O caryatid O my katydid,
did you once carry my world or my cross?
Look, my legs swing one across the other,

as a kind of cross, a cross I could bear,
walking across town or swinging my foot,
or a cross, as I said, that would bear me—

my own long legs that were holding me up.
There were days, I said, when I didn't care,
either standing so still or leaping up.

Renaissance

I meant I was and I had always been
the thing I was, though I wanted to be
another version of what being was.

Ha! That would be a busman's holiday,
or getting a buzz on, we used to say,
or borrowing from the bees or the birds

(*and to do that to birds was why she came*),
doing or being, been there and done that.
But it didn't mean lunching on thrushes

and swallowing songs from a songbird's throat,
or else driving in the back of the bus
or else being driven from up ahead.

Drive yourself to distraction was a thought
related to both being and doing.
These old thoughts were coming to me in droves—

not to make too much of a metaphor.
But there was no new news under the sun,
no new news and even fewer songs;

maybe newness was what I didn't want,
maybe only a dose of otherness,
which didn't mean death or eternity.

O wing O wing, and all the flourishes
arranged so neatly on my shoulder blades,
exotic and ornate on my plain back,

and as rideable as a Persian rug . . .
It was laughable but reassuring,
this tender fillip of the Renaissance,

Filippo Lippi painting in the wings,
a flitter or a flutter now and then,
and the announcement of a coming thing.

Bomb

Was I playing it in the hope of joy,
play it as it lays, as someone said,
playing it down or else playing it up,

or was there some other raison d'être,
some other raisin drying in the sun,
or some other reason under the sun.

Please excuse my French, was there a reason
for being and doing anything else,
dreaming or dying for anything else.

"Be content with lack of misery"
was a kind of motto for some of us,
a kind of bonbon or a platitude,

or a kind of candy for a sucker
when what you need is a drink of sense,
the mot juste and a drink of joy or juice.

Drink up, drink up, or else drink it down,
have you ever pondered the difference?
Not a bon mot or else a play on words

but a choice between rising and falling.
Or lay it aside, play it as you can,
when what you need is some balm for the heart,

or else a pillow for your pretty head,
or a pill, or a grape plucked from the vine.
Maybe a surge, a surfeit or an urge

or something urgent in the argument,
as though reasoning could be part of it:
some say a surge of joy might be killing.

Acrolith

I had been hoping for a change of scene,
surfing the centuries for something new,
like a new head for an ancient body

or a new body for an ancient head
dredged from the sea or a sarcophagus,
or like a new tooth for a tired smile,

iconic or else maybe ironic,
in gold or silver, in plaster or stone,
some metallurgy or mimicry,

a simulacrum or a simile,
like deadheading a favorite rose
or else starting again from the sourcebook.

Sorcerer! Will you give me back my source,
give me a head or let me get ahead;
maybe only a shift of mood or heart,

a goblet of wine and a gulp of air,
a milestone on the road to Nirvana.
Wasn't Nirvana the goal of the nerves

or a hill town on the outskirts of Rome,
a headstone on the highway to heaven?
All this searching for a surge of surprise,

when all I found was as old as the hills.
Surgeon! A splurge, a surfeit or an urge
to bring me to my senses or stun them,

some salvage from the ruin of myself,
some saving grace, a means of saving face—
the face-lift of a Roman fantasy.

Head

No, I was thinking I would lose my head
when there was the emperor's man, and thwack—
it wasn't my hat that was missing.

I was a sister or I was a saint,
maybe a gilded statue of Venus,
sporting a halo or wearing a hat,

blood on my bosom or no blood at all,
gilding a lily or a gala gown;
I was the garderobe or the avant-garde

with the guards at my back in the palace.
What was a bust without a head on it,
what was a dress without a girl in it,

a dress or a bag, a drape or a rag.
Dear Lesbia and poor fat Drusilla,
an emporium of décolletages

or a model of empiricism.
No, "please save me" wasn't a noble thought,
but save my face, at least that act of grace!

All this was heady, which didn't mean smart;
it was the foam or the fizz, or the fat,
the cut of the gown, the slash of the neck.

Oh god, how I wanted to dance and dance,
dress in a lily, shake myself silly.
The thought wriggled up, but my head was gone.

It could be me or my image in stone.
It might be a headstone or a hanger,
a headache maybe, or a hangover.

Colosseum

That was the blood again, the selfsame spot
that had to go—which didn't mean the rose,
though blood and a rose could share a color.

It rose to my face, as a blush would do,
for showing you that I was what I was.
I was the empress or else the goddess

or the servant of my sensual thoughts,
and I threw all my meat to the lions
to be eaten alive or lionized.

A colossal mess I made of my life,
in the flesh and also in the round;
this was the essence of colosseum,

the museum of my colossal shame,
where I mused on the blood sport of it all,
where I longed for the lust of the lions.

Here was my game, the name of my sin,
for I never threw men to the lions
or rose from my lair or ate men like air,

or pearls to the pigs, though I tossed a rose
to the crowds and begged them to spare my life,
dominion and dungeon of the senses,

and all the beauty and the blasphemy.
Petals, petals, scattering from the stands
where only vestals were allowed to sit,

having tended the flame for all of us.
Here, I knew, was the empire of my soul
showing on my face as I turned to you.

Veronica (Vera Icon)

I was walking on Via Veneto.
Va-va-voom! he said, and I laughed out loud:
it was all in the verve of the gesture.

I was a green-eyed blonde, I was a girl.
Vainglory! Will you give me some of it,
garrulous, god-struck, full of vinegar.

This might have been a visionary stance,
a revision of Isis and Venus,
reversion to a vision of grandeur,

or desire in a raw and vital state,
another variant of verismo
and as vivid as a green valentine.

Viva! Some green blood running in my veins,
te quiero verde (I want you green),
which didn't mean I want you virtuous

if virtue meant veiling your truer thoughts.
Or maybe virtue was Veronica,
an adventure in the vernacular,

passing her handkerchief, tossing her cape.
One was a swinger, one was a saint,
one was devoid of all vanity and

one was standing in the path of the bull:
it was all in the quest for victory.
There was vanitas, there was veritas,

I hoped I had both guts and godliness.
Some of us had more and some had less—
this was the true truth we were green about.

Sine Qua Non

I was wandering in a quandary
and never without a qualm or a pang,
and thinking of taking a quantum leap

out of my quondam life and into yours.
Not, I didn't say, my goddamn life, I
said my own life I didn't care to live.

Not to be quarrelsome, quote me on this;
who were you anyway, who have you been,
my quotient or quorum of joy or jazz.

I said your life, which was a better one,
or would have been, dear love, with me in it.
My sine qua non, where did you wander?

I took a gander, and that was my life
(oh where was Juno when I needed her),
a quiet gamble on my golden eggs,

on the qui vive for a kiss or a hand,
asking the question, the querulous one,
like who lives and who loves and how do they.

Quo vadis, as history often asked;
the answer, always, was I'm going back,
looking for a goose, a lamb or a duck,

a croon or a cluck, a quid for my quo.
This was quackery, I mean a bad fix,
dumb luck, my destiny or a dumb fuck,

many beautiful fucks, quote me on this,
meaning fucking you again and again
and being fucked by you, which was the same.

Trauma

I was trammeled, I thought, by tragedy,
oh what, something long ago, some travail
of my soul or my body, or of both.

The "little tragedies of daily life"
tremoring through me—tremor wasn't a verb,
tra-la-la wasn't either, or trial,

though they trailed through my life, didn't they,
a tracery of tears, a track of woes.
Woes, woes, ten little fingers and toes,

decades of them, this deed, that distortion,
a tort against the treasured harmony.
A twist or a twirl, a tic, a tic-tac-toe,

thrumming on the synapses, drumming out
a threnody of threats and tears, a thought-
torture, love, love, a tiny tortured heart.

My heart, my own little tap-tapping heart,
my tapped-out heart, their testament to me,
a test of wills, or a test of my will,

my willingness, my wish to weather on.
Oh waves, waves, all the ripples and rhythms,
the rituals of walking and reaching,

the verbiage, the verb-thoughts, try this, try that;
the rites of therapy and talking trash,
the tapestry of tears, the truth-trapeze.

But did I want the truth? Try me, I said.
This is, this was, this should never have been;
reason, thought-treason and some truisms.

John

Oh give me joy, give me a job in life,
not jobbing or jokes or hobnobbery,
love as a job, not a hand job; a life,

said Freud, is a job and a love. Oh John,
join me forever in my jamboree.
This, after all, was my jubilee year.

Or was I jinxed, was I jinxed or jerked
or deviled by some inner jinx or jive;
some deviled eggs and a slice of *jambon*.

I thought my eggs were maybe too deviled.
Was he hobbled by the gist or the junk,
a job-lot attitude toward choosing joy,

was any girl as good as another?
A Janus look, I mean facing two ways,
toward love and away judiciously;

or Juan, a kind of dungeon of love
(oh be jolly oh be jaunty and brave).
Now I was thinking I would egg him on,

but I got egg on my face, as always.
The mumbo-jumbo, the jumble, the mum,
mumbling love, may I give you my jewel,

the Juliet from the Ethiope's ear,
my lips, my laughter, my adjurations.
Leave your door ajar, and I'll come in.

Let us adjourn, I mean call it a day,
or a night, do let us call it a night
while the jasmine still blooms in the garden.

Graffito
after "Amat qui scribet"

FOR KRISTINA MILNOR

Would you engrave my body with your hands?
I would be grateful—I would be so glad—
if you would etch me for eternity

with all the vicissitudes of your hand
and some vision and some vulgarity.
Let me lie here now in a dusty box

with all your vim and love inscribed in me,
may I be scratched here, and then gather dust.
Oh let me first be loved, and then be lost.

Who reads is fucked, and I read you right out,
let me read you again all over me.
Who criticizes, sucks—or so he said—

we know it was a man who wrote these things
with a stylus or maybe with a stick
on a gray wall—on yellow or blue—

or on Neapolitan red or pink—
with a pocketknife or maybe a pick.
Engrave me also with some gravitas

and some caritas and some veritas.
He who writes, loves—caring, grave and true.
Write me with grit and grace, may I say this,

here where the graph may be the holy grail.
Let's grapple with the beasts—that is, *the bears*—
let them *tear us*—write it!—*from limb to limb.*

Amourette

It lasted many moons—in fact decades—
but, you know, never morphed into marriage.
Slow amour, as slow as a snail,

and as armored as an armadillo.
Was imperfect love a peccadillo,
or wasn't it love, this purgatory;

in the end I think I was mortified.
Speaking of *petite mort*, there was also
petty murder. O ambrosia. I was

amortized, you know, or slowly murdered
while waiting for a metamorphosis.
It was disarming that it was over.

There was harm in him, and a dose of smarm—
that I wasn't dead was the miracle.
I wasn't quite dead, but almost, you know,

arm over arm with my malefactor.
And, you know, alarmingly amorous.
In marital, martial and lunar law

the dead girl can't marry her mortician.
No one was left but the Necromancer,
not the Romancer and not Amore,

something like heavens to murgatory,
and all the morphology of remorse.
To think purgatory led to heaven!

An armchair, *mon cher*, not a chariot,
all that old passion put out to pasture
for grazing, you know, on "past" memories.

Fix

Fixable, it never was. I knew that.
Or too late to fix by the time I knew.
Fox hunting, a red fox lost in a fog.

Field—fog—fuck. Oh love, was this fantasy.
Va fan culo. As always, go get fucked,
when, after all, that was what I wanted.

My love, a love of fun, a fantasy,
my own fox tail switching in the fog. A
fierce desire, a red tail lost in the snow,

red, white, and the gray branches overhead.
Filigree, fond searches—some fact-finding.
It might be better not to have a fact,

better a totem or a factotum,
an emblem of the general desire,
a handyman or a fox of all trades,

to fix me this or maybe fetch me that—
maybe some thunder or a fundament.
Though there was rarely thunder in a fog.

Fogged in, foxed. No, I wasn't faking it.
Fox, fox—they used to call me that—fine girl—
fetching—they once said that too. Oh love, love,

fetch me a forkful or a fingerful,
a figment or a fig, fetch me a fix.
Oh damn foxation and thunderation,

expectations and fixabilities.
But then, after all, this was my whole life:
I had a thunderous desire to be.

Obelisk

I do believe I was never loved. I
was never loved. An outright blasphemy,
saying so point-blank and out of the blue,

an observation I wanted to make,
maybe too obvious to bother with,
or a bagatelle—too banal to tell—

one little beauty who was never loved,
as blue as a bag lady and as black
as the occupant of an oubliette,

maybe an octopus but not of bliss.
I was blame-emblazoned, my obloquy,
and as bellicose as an obelisk,

as black as a sack, as sick as a sock,
this blah-blah-blah, the soul of lullaby.
Obliteration, that old oration,

blanketing my blue soul, my blue, my soul.
I gave you this oblation to belief,
or maybe obviating disbelief,

and not a ball—no, never a ballet.
I gave you my bold hope, my openness,
as oblong as a long embattled day,

I got a bellyful, I got a beaut—
not to be oblique: a banana fish.
You know you blasted me a round of blanks.

But after all, what was believable
if not my own blue soul on a black day,
when all the beloved were so blasé.

Chagrin

It wasn't the life I would have wanted,
had I known what sort of life I did want,
as if anyone ever knew; though I

did know. Everyone had her shadow life,
her should-have life, the life she should have had,
all those thoughts sharp-sharking into her soul,

all those doodles on the skin of the day.
The shame, that this had been and this had not,
could-should, kowtowing to the life of should,

the shock, let's say, of seeing it had passed,
the chagrin, let's say, the savage chagrin
that this was what it was, et cetera,

who did I think I was, et cetera,
the queen of Sheba in her shantytown,
or Shirley in her temple (*such a doll*),

or Scheherazade waking to the day—
not Sylvia, not the sylvan huntress.
The whole shebang was a shambles, hello,

shanghaiing my wishes, shout it out, shout,
those stories of what was and never was,
love, voyage, give me succor—sugar—suck—

hushing the heart and shushing the senses.
Hello, day, shake the sheets out, wake the day.
Cheers! (As I said this I was choking up.)

The challenge of cheerfulness—hello, charm—
charade and charm, chameleon, cameo.
I saw the dawn and fell into a hush.

Sybil

I thought I would, yes—or no, I wouldn't—
surrender to these thoughts, this thought-surfeit.
In the service of survival, I thought

I would live on the surface of my life,
or surf, let's say, on the waves of my life
—so fun—and so forth—alas—selah—

Some sophisticated sortilege for
shooing off the insinuating snakes.
O Sybil, will you save me from my self-

surrender, and my sacrifice to—what—?
Sulfuric vapors at the mouth of hell.
In what sense did Sappho survive her life?

She was slain by her life, as we all are.
Let me safari to the farthest shore,
let me hunt sapphires and never suffer.

This weird, solemn world, my word and my way,
this savage world and my self-slavery.
A zephyr blowing—a slow fire—the fat

soprano singing shrilly in her cave—
zaftig—oh so fat—inwardly a sylph.
Sympathetic symphony of sad facts.

Enough of this slavish salivation!
Let me pour out a lavish libation,
let me simmer saffron in a slow stew,

some salve or salvation for Sylvia.
O Sybil, show me something I don't know,
surprise me with some savvy funny news!

Cant

I said I could never live here, and I
never could, but I did for two decades—
I had fallen into a decadence.

No, not a cadence, though that too could fall,
darkly—ever so darkly—through a glass,
or a mirror or a dirty window

barred like a skeleton, barred like a cage.
Not as though I didn't care—I did care.
I had been carping on the debacle

for most of ten years in the candlelight,
the decorum of the core of the deed,
decked in desire, here in my dark cave—

decorated with me, or with my core,
the dark card of the dark lass and lady,
dandling on her lap my own life—my life—

while I combed through the old crowns and papers.
It was tiny but cavernous, it was
cadaverous, it was my catacomb.

But could I be decanted from this jar?
Cant! Cant! The cant of I can't—no, I can't—
comb out my hair, climb out of my lair and

dance with the wind in the dandelions.
If the door was ajar, would I go out,
a cat darting her head around the door

(carpe diem, carry away the day).
A canticle of anticipation,
some dandelion wine and a draft of air.

Petrarch

Oh me, who was my enemy: only
me. I was enacting an anarchy
of me when what I know I needed was

an artfulness. The conundrum of my
innerness—or the eardrum of my me,
always listening to my inner hum.

Oh heart, a sense of humor please, a sense
of inner human humor, a rumor
or a ruffling of happiness. Drum roll:

the conundrum of my cunt (*so sorry*),
the drumming in that inner room—alarm!
Disarm the scaffolding—O arcanum—

and unfold the arch, my architecture,
all the textures of my folded temple
and all the ruffles of an ecstasy.

A penny arcade and some archery,
and a parakeet and a parapet,
the sky above in every color and

a carpet changing colors with the sky.
Pet, pet—could I whisper it to myself
while Petrarch was whispering to Laura

out there on the autoroute to Arqua?
Could I save myself with an arch remark,
could I call myself out on the carpet?

Sistine

I was moving from crisis to crisis
all through my life, with a few calm days
between them like a caress or a charm

descending unexpected from above.
Up there, god's hand was pointing toward Adam
when it could be turning toward the Sybil.

Who cared for love when there was wisdom?
All that stuff in my satchel full of scrolls—
a chrysanthemum or a chrysalid,

for crying out loud, wasn't that enough.
Crystallizing the future as an eye,
lifting up the future as an eyelid,

always gazing with a critical eye.
But how sad not to have loved the Sun God
when he might have given me all I wished.

What was so bad about a night of sex?
Here I was, hanging shriveled in my cage,
saying I want to die—want to be dead.

Oh cry sister—or else just suck it up—
or spend some time with Savonarola.
Maybe it was just those sulfuric fumes

rising from deep in the Stygian swamp
that caused my sad moment of misjudgment.
When all the while a mere stanza or two

might have saved the day, saying I love you
—eternities ago—or maybe not.
Or was there still time for some kiss-and-tell,

or some scissoring schism of the heart.
Come down to Cumae and open my cage.
Sad! I had forever but not a kiss.

Song

I said I couldn't love and it was true,
not a ploy, or coy. I couldn't love or
sing. Not canti or canzoni or chants

or airs—not—I could do sex but not
without love, and I couldn't love so I
couldn't do sex. Oy, oy, as the Jews say,

no love and no song, that means no joy.
Happiness, you once said, is not a goal,
it's a happenstance. It happens to some

and not to others. It may have happened
sometime to Mina Loy, or to Myrna,
or to Terry Malloy, but not to me.

Life without love is life without love, as
dry as a stick; it's sick, though saying so,
my love, is cloying. It's not worth a stick.

La, la, I sometimes almost broke into
song—a broken song, could you call it that?
We were drinking rob roys! Those were the nights.

I had inner singing and inner love
but not for me, not for you, I had love
for a boy I once knew but not for you,

never a loyal and unalloyed joy.
This was my stance, and maybe my stanza,
and this was the substance of my romance.

I never could love, now I was oily,
ogling their pants, their hearts, and their hairlines.
Oh how annoying, a blonde with no beau,

an old girl with no toy and no ally.
Oh boy, boy, I know I broke your heart
with my broken song. I know I was wrong.

Tara

Scarlett, I always knew we were the same,
but who was I talking to, saying this,
to you, Scarlett, to you, but who are you,

turning to Tara as I turn to me,
looking I guess for some help from the land,
when the land of course was only my heart,

or hoping for a turn for the better
while turning the soil, when for all that time
the dirt of my soul was talking back. Crows!

They seemed to be everywhere, crowding in,
stalking the furrows whenever they could,
going up one row and then down the next.

We were sumptuous girls, belles of the ball,
a harem of men hanging on our skirts
as long as they did, and then they were gone

harum-scarum, having crowed to our hearts.
So if I were you I would sell myself
for a house or a heart—be a harlot!

With a lot of hair and those freckled hands?
Starlet, will you lend me a barn or a stair,
but I am you and I don't guess I can.

I might buy up a nightclub in Harlem
and listen alone to some scatty jazz.
Scarred, would you say, or scared? Oh my land,

I'm not sure I can scare up a sale;
did I once tell you this was harrowing?
There were horrors and then there were horrors

and no, this was not really one of them.
I guess I'll take a furlough from this field
and hang up my old dress on your scarecrow.

Tempest

I had a flash of insight: there weren't
all that many years left in my life, it
was now or never or never or now.

Full fathom five my father lay but I—
I was standing in the eye of the storm
and it was seeing me or me it, or

neither of us was seeing the other.
I'm telling you I needed a sea change
or to see some change, if change could be seen.

I was just a tempest in a teapot
but I liked my tea, I liked me; my life
was the life I wanted to like. It was

tempting to feel there was something out there,
a flash of lightning or a jag of truth.
Here was the pathetic fallacy and

here was Ariel in his gust of air,
spinning and turning and dancing in air.
But I was slim-bodied and full-breasted,

and tired of my island, my eye, my land,
and no, I didn't need a fallacy!
And no more pathos! (It was *pathetic*.)

I needed a phallus—but not on me—
and not in the elements or heavens.
A flash in the flesh and not in the pan!

And now Miranda stepped into the sun
and gazing away at her strange new world,
poured out some tea for you, her prince, for you.

Goose

Was it over now, I wanted to know,
was it gone, you know, was the game up,
or was I still game, speaking of pheasants,

was I a partridge or a parakeet.
Was I simmering or no, was I stewed
in my own juices, or was my goose cooked.

This was *the wild goose on the barren branch*.
Got your goose, I think someone once said,
and yes, mine was gotten. But not the one

that laid the golden egg. No, not that egg.
Not as good as gold or as gold as straw,
and not the needle in the golden stack.

Not passing through the eye, or through the gates
of horn or gold, or through the pearly ones.
Was I saying I wanted to be dead

or just saying I wanted some heaven—
the rich man in the eye of the needle
or else a dance on the head of a pin

or just a rich man, thank you, that heaven,
or else five golden rings instead of one.
Looking for a partridge in a pear tree

or only a pear, or maybe a pearl
in my oyster or an oyster in my soup.
Looking for a pear in a partridge tree

or some golden eggs left on the beanstalk.
Was I as good as gold, or was I old,
could I lay some gold myself, could I live?

Starlings

All winter I watched the swarms of starlings
swooping in the northern sky like cast nets
or some foreign alphabets flying loose

and returning and rushing out again.
I wanted to live the life I desired,
as we all did, I think, our one desire,

wanting to do what we wanted to do,
sweeping and then spreading and turning back.
A flood of arrows, dare-arrows, daring to hope,

never horizontals or verticals,
not a straight arrow or as the crow flew,
though life, I think, looked daggers at me,

daring me write this letter now to you,
scratching the sky with a row of my words
(*those letters sent to him that lives away*).

Look me daggers, love, stare me in the eye,
dare me to love you and I'll dare you back.
Darling, I will say, my starling, my crow—

no, not a thrush as the century turned,
though I felt a rush looking at the sky
and all the devastations of desire,

as staggering as ever—startling, true,
or dulled, I think, by the drift of the years
or the drag of the years dragging me back

through the smudges of my alphabets,
cirrus clouds like rags cleaning up the sky
and the vast waste of my wasted desire.

Armor

I am nothing if I'm not a lover,
a loved love; we are nothing if not that;
I wasn't but *I am* if you'll let me

be your amphora and your amulet.
For there were days to live and days to love,
meaning there was still a lot of life left

for us, for me if you were there in it,
and maybe you would be and maybe not.
This was the question for me, of our amour,

our armor, the mind and body that we
wore, or were, the armor of our arms and
more, the morphology of our amour.

There was only this life, this love of ours,
together as we were and as we are,
armed and firing in the line of fire.

We were amateurs in the art of love,
you *ami ami* and me, you and me.
Here was shape-shifting in the truest form,

meaning more than form and more than us,
rubbing the stones in our pockets for luck.
Those lucky in love were lucky in life.

A great view of the city lay below
this statue to our metamorphosis,
a monument, my love, to love not war—

ambling arm in arm, drinking up the night.
Think if they made statues to love heroes
returning from the Campus Martius.

Park of the Doria Pamphilj

I know I was startled to feel like this,
staring straight into the eye of the storm,
the stone pines turning toward me and away—

stands of them standing, and then bending back,
and showing the filigree of their crowns,
the lace of their brains against the gray sky,

brandishing themselves like many giant wands,
or pinwheels or kaleidoscopes, gray-black,
green-black, showing the inside of their minds,

and not colliding though it seemed they could,
and ruffling the sky with their big green hair.
I was there, I'm telling you, I was there,

and I saw it like a cocktail party:
we were all holding up our martinis
in long-stemmed glasses, looking at our minds,

as wet and dreamy as a stormy sky,
pining for a departure or a part,
a promenade through the ancient city.

I was a madwoman wearing a green hat,
I was a maenad or a martinet,
or a mannequin waiting to be dressed,

and leaning toward my friend the skeleton,
a scope or a decision, or a hope,
pinning me to a purpose or a part,

eliding me with something in this life,
as lean as a stick, reaching toward the sky,
some skeleton or rorschach of a thought,

a potato print or a pantomime:
and being one wanderer, long I stood,
going somewhere while rooted to the ground.

Pantheon

If I had known the pleasure principle,
how different all those years would have been,
all those years I spent plaintive and pleading,

but that was plain pain, that was the pure stuff;
could I sing it as a psalm or a hymn,
a sigh to god or to some other one

to look this way, not that way, and soothe me.
Forsooth and so forth, it did not occur.
I was forsaken, and not for my sake—

for whose sake I'll never know, believe me.
Force of habit, or force of not having,
or perforce it had to be, and it was.

Or peremptory, on the part of who?
Meaning who was it who picked out my part
instead of giving it to someone else,

or phase, passage, it could never be known.
Though pass me a pill, or give me your hand,
hand me a pillow or else a haven,

or read my palm and tell me what you see:
I see a palm at the end of my mind,
swaying like an arm, waving like a hand,

the print of a palm or else a blueprint,
a pantheon or a panopticon,
or the prison or prism of myself,

meaning the one view or all of the views,
or else the one god or all of the gods,
and none of them explained what had happened.

Acknowledgments

The author thanks the editors of the journals in which these poems first appeared:

American Academy in Rome Society of Fellows News: "Head"
The Antioch Review: "Cross," "Lessons"
Harvard Divinity Bulletin: "Renaissance"
The Kenyon Review: "Park of the Doria Pamphilj," "Starlings"
Literary Imagination: "Cant," "Petrarch"
Nuovi Argomenti: "Green Market," as *"Mercato delle verdure,"*
    translated into Italian by Damiano Abeni
Southwest Review: "Grotesque"
The Threepenny Review: "Acrolith"

She also thanks the American Academy of Arts and Letters and the American Academy in Rome for the John Guare Rome Prize Fellowship, during which most of these poems were written.

A NOTE ABOUT THE AUTHOR

Sarah Arvio was born in 1954 and grew up near New York City. For
Visits from the Seventh (2002), her first book of poems, she won the Rome
Prize and a John Simon Guggenheim Memorial Foundation fellowship.
Poems in that volume were awarded *The Paris Review*'s Bernard F. Con-
ners Prize and *Poetry*'s Frederick Bock Prize. Arvio works as a translator
for the United Nations.

A NOTE ON THE TYPE

The text of this book was set in Van Dijck, a modern revival of a type-
face attributed to the Dutch master punch cutter Christoffel van Dyck,
c. 1606–1669. The revival was produced by the Monotype Corporation
in 1937–1938 with the assistance, and perhaps over the objection, of the
Dutch typographer Jan van Krimpen. Never in wide use, Monotype
Van Dijck nonetheless has the familiar and comfortable qualities of the
types of William Caslon, who used the original Van Dijck as the model
for his famous type.

Composed by Stratford Publishing Services,
Brattleboro, Vermont

Printed and bound by United Book Press,
Baltimore, Maryland